First published in 2023 by GWP
Greg Williams Photography
Lower Ground Floor
34 North Row
London W1K 6DG

ISBN: 978-1-8382424-1-1
10 9 8 7 6 5 4 3 2 1
001 – September 2023

Cover image by Olly & Suzi
Designed by Mike Bone
Printed in the UK

Printed on FSC® certified paper.

A CIP record for this book
is available from the British Library.

DRAW
OF THE
WILD

A poet's wanderings
and wonderings in wilderness

OLLY WILLIAMS

with Foreword by Hussain Manawer
and Preface by Greg Williams

FOREWORD

Hussain Manawer

Poet and Sunday Times Bestselling Author

Hailing from a British Pakistani background in East London, venturing out and exploring the great outdoors and Mother Nature wasn't something that was truly encouraged; in school for a few hours a week it was, but it wasn't anything more than that.

Now I'm not sure if that's a cultural thing or something to do with living within an inner city. But what I do know is that my grandparents came to the United Kingdom from Kashmir, Mirpur. And with many recent trips to Pakistan, the mountainous grounds of the space forever inspire me to reconnect with the powers and beauty of the outdoors. However this inspiration quickly fades, as I walk the concrete cobbled paths of London town.

Recently, I was exceptionally fortunate to come across the great soul of the Poet, Writer, Explorer and Artist Olly Williams, and having sat with him on a bench outdoors it truly was a love at first write moment. Two men, meeting at a garden party, pouring their hearts out on their love of poetry, art, the planet, humanity and everything else in between.

Reading his poetry as it effortlessly fell down the page, instantly encapsulated a part of me that needed to be touched. I looked up at him and said nothing, as nothing needed to be said. After a short silence I thanked him for showing me and asked if there was more. And more there was.

Not only did his words make me think, they made me feel. I began feeling the essence of what I have been voluntarily depriving myself of: the beauty, the elegance and the wonderment of Mother Nature and her species. A piece from Olly's collection entitled *Green Hills* has a line within it that sticks with me: 'And in so doing you, to Me, become sacred.'

Olly, your work has inspired me to get out, to move, to sit, to feel, to be at one with nature, and in doing so, God willing, become at one with myself. Thank you my friend.

The mental health of the world is in much need of human artistic connection now more than ever. The combination of lyricism, heart, art, compassion and passion within Olly's work tells me one thing: within the pages of *Draw Of The Wild*, there is love amongst the chaos after all.

Hussain Manawer

PREFACE

Greg Williams
Photographer

There are many comparisons between our planet's impending environmental catastrophe and the Great War. One I often think of, is that of power-hungry men causing the death of the very thing we all love the most – our younger generations.

Over the past thirty-five years Olly has been a witness on the environmental front line; in the jungles, deserts, oceans, and in the Arctic, where it is most clear to see the recent devastating changes to the natural world that he loves so much.

I compare his work to that of the Great War poets, and the message is just as important.

Within these pages you will find quieter personal poems, but at their heart the works collected in this book are a passionate plea to preserve nature.

My brother Olly's artistry has transferred seamlessly from his paintbrush to the written word – only starting to write poetry in the past couple of years, it has poured out of him, and is presented here for the first time in the pages of *Draw of the Wild*.

Greg Williams

Dark Ocean

White is gone
forever here.
Dark ocean greedy,
for the sun.

No bergs float,
the seals have left,
Nanook,
fierce myth.

Once mighty
Orca pod
resigned
to Saga.

As tide
devoid
of herring ball,
krill and the cod,

an empty
maelstrom
lifeless
broils.

On land,
once frozen,
Muskeg lakes like
virus spread,

tannin
waters, gassy
bubbling
as intoxicated

Boreal spruce
do drunken
fall and so,
it goes

all of it,
the Arctic
melting, drip
by drip.

Author's note: The poems in this book are presented in alphabetical order, with the exception of *Dark Ocean* and *Words* which open and close this collection of poems by means of prologue/epilogue. I simply wish that each poem be stumbled upon, transmitting their unique signals, as each wild encounter was gifted me.

POEMS

A Brother Lost

Swaying willows betray your thundering wake,
crashing through waters
red with salmon running.
The blushing, eviscerated hulks
scattered scaly on the shale,
indents of still-warm day bed flattened in the sedge.
Purple blueberry scat steaming
beside high-country trails,
your five-toed track, vital evidence in the mud.
Gouged bark, worn smooth on favourite rubbing pine,
replete with coarse tufts of brown bear hair,
encrusted golden in pungent sap.
Your hoarse moan echoing,
through misty stands of hemlock,
alder and the cottonwoods,
over snowy alps and down through ancient rainforest glades,
across black-sand beaches, as giants amble, nonchalant
mining for prized razor clams.
Wilderness no longer truly wild, if we a brother lost.

Amongst Holly

Your berries shout
Above the forest's dead,
Plump clustered, jewels
Drenched, deep in bloody red.

No other spray so gently
Pricks in pain,
No waxy green, so glistens
In the rain.

Leaf of chieftain's wreath
Claws against my arm,
Yet spiky omen,
Does, to me no harm.

So now, I navigate
The path unseen.
Amongst Holly,
Eternal, evergreen.

Aurora

For Peggy

A darkness fell,
Aurora's
Emerald green
Came smoothly,

Emanating
Within the starry night
Crackling hues
Of pink evolving,

Melding, dazzling,
Black spruce silhouetted
Against slow show
Of northern light.

Baltic Swans

Across from
Skansen, mallard
Bobbed
As friends talked
Happily,
Sun shimmering,
Illuminating
Baltic swans,
Their plumage
Soft, necks
Elegantly
Folded into wing,
Shielding.

Bare Larch

Today, Larch
Stand almost bare.
Smudge of yellow
Halo, above the
Evergreens.

A week ago,
These trees had
Danced. Vibrant, glowing
Colours overflowing.
Now leeched

Of glory,
Mere memory remains,
As pledge, for another year.
Before autumnal storms
When gold adorns,
And Larch, once more, take fire.

Beast

Pushing through
the clawing trees,
a heft of beast
crashed ominously.

As moon grew full,
I stumbled on
until dark pool
before me shone.

Approaching water's
edge I peered
and what leered back
I truly feared.

Blue

As night fell across
The jetty, cerulean
Waters shimmered,
Sharky
In abundance.

Here, under star-filled
Skies, baby killers
Patrolled a blue
So dazzlingly bright
As to be worshipful.

Bracken

I swam through a sea
of green. Pushing against a
tide of pliant stems.

The deeper I went,
the closer I felt to the
forest. To nature.

Calm

Sometimes, things unsettle,
not one of us exempt.
Life just throws us curved balls,
stress, my detriment.

Walking makes me calmer
through forests, fields and hills,
senses strangely focused,
helps negate my ills.

Fear is always lurking.
But so is nature's balm.
So, I must keep on walking
To renovate my calm.

Caribou Defeated

At 'Place to Seine'
We found them;
Herd starved, piled
Emaciated.

Lichens locked
Within refrozen glaze,
Sacred Porcupine
Caribou

Defeated.
Not by nature's hand,
But wind-blown,
Man-made melting, freezing.

Collaboration

For Fitzy

Sensing. That is what
I see you do. Your hazel
Eyes scanning, ears large,

Nose deciphering
Emanation. Even your
Elegant paws sense

Resonation – from
Deep within the ochre soil.
Blessed therefore is

Your gift to perceive.
Whether waft, squeak or scamper,
Predator, prey or

Fat sod that enters
The sacred space between. And
In that instant, you

Know me better than
I could ever know myself.
My total being,

Even intention.
All I am and all I will
Ever be. Only

Then do you share what
You have learned. A whirring, now
Punctuated with

Sneeze-like guttural
Bark, each member of your tribe
Alerted as bright

Random patches of
Black, white and yellow the hue
Of sunflowers morph

Into raggedy
Cerberus. Now are you as
One. In that moment

I consider your
Congregation. Surely is
Collaboration

Not your sharpest tool?
Yes, your legs are lithe. Torso
Whip, your muzzle broad,

Your teeth all lethal
Business. Yet certain I am
These attributes do

Not define the point
Of 'you'. You are not awesome
Like the tawny king

I have witnessed you
Defy. Neither, lonesome like
The leopard. What

You Are is vital.
To the Game relentlessly
You pursue and to

Your wild lands. All I
Fear lost without you doing
What only you do.

I wonder if you
Innately know the part you
Play? Your role in the

Survival of life?
Like wind running through wild grasses,
And the hot sky above,

To me you are both
Sermon and scripture. The God
You serve, mightier

Than comprehension.
Oh, Wild dog! I will miss you
Each and every day.

Coral Gardens

For Suzi

As we ascended,
Fears confronted
Coral gardens soothed,
Wide eyes with colour.

Here we simply floated.
Weightless, transfixed,
Trigger fish darting
Parrots, bats,
Toothy rabbits too
And there, our air

Almost done –
Feasting on anemone,
A turtle nonchalantly lunched
Light dappling its shell.

This magical reef
Spelt home, not to us,
But coral's abundance
Protected by waves
Strong currents, tropical storms
Yet still, so vulnerable.

Death

Descending verdant ridge of staggered
Doum and Miombo thick,
with scores of mumbling buff,

we emerged cautiously, onto arid plain
and there, discovered sprawled Impala slain.
Sun baked in the mud.

The skeletal remains shrouded in
dried parchment of its hide,
appeared frozen

in a single, graceful stride.
We wondered at what beast might
have wrought death upon this antelope?

Or whether it had simply laid to rest,
a life well lived, never to regain its feet.
What we understood, beyond a doubt,

was nothing in its earthly core had
been wasted, out here in the bush.
This creature had served others, with its life.

And reminded us of our mortality.
Not fearful of the inevitable,
just grateful for the now: heat on our backs

and sweat on brow.
Intensely prepared
for dangers, lurking.

Deity

Up ahead, deep in the trees,
dressed in Adidas shorts
and ragged Arsenal tee,
the Piaroa toted
his parang as a commuter
would an umbrella.

I was struck how elegantly
the hunter moved.
At one with his forest,
as sweating we staggered.
Until our tracker signalled
for us to stop, dead.

He bent, and cut a strand of vine,
and on his belly crawled
to the base of rotting dead fall.
With a grin, he twirled the spindly
Liana strand delicately, between thumb and forefinger,
in and out of a fist-sized hole.

We watched entranced
as an apparition loomed,
in the dark entrance of the nest.
Then the Goliath spider emerged,
twelve inches wide
in unsettling scamper.

Dappled light danced
upon the ginger velvet of its abdomen.
Its head the size of a sand dollar,
bejewelled with all sensing eyes and terrible
mandibles replete with inch-long stabbing
fangs that now latched with fury to the infuriating vine.

Instantly we felt the primal trigger
that all primates innately understand.
To beware of spiders,
both small and godlike.
Then the spider raced,
eight articulated legs frenetic

before a lighting swipe
with sharpened stake,
pinned vast arachnid
remorselessly –
yet with profound love and deflated hiss
to the spongy jungle floor.

In shock, we contemplated
the murdered deity.
A predator we had come so far to meet,
but Piaroa aimed to share
their shamanic delicacy,
roasted until blacked

in shroud of neon green banana leaf
and eagerly consumed.
The white meat, crab-like and delicious,
as we sat cross-legged by bush TV
till not one morsel remained…
So, no!

Zero outside judgement here.
Just simple comprehension of when in Rome.
Oh Orinoco, our wild and jungly,
yet most sacred home
where venerated creatures roam and
gods, on this occasion, became our dinner too.

Dew

Dew   like glass
    slung,

From damp branch
Reflects trees,
Magnifies
My fingertip.
Once touched,

Drops.

Draw of the Wild

For Henry

What draws the wild in you?
If you close your eyes.
Is it the great forests that you see?
Or treeless realms?
The windswept Arctic tundra,
broiling desert sands, cloud-swept
Himalayan peaks, the oceans deep,
or the riot of sultry, jungly lands?

Maybe you are drawn to wild, majestic beasts –
the big mammalian stuff?
The moan of tiger, roaring lion,
the great bear's cough?
The collaboration of wild dog,
the truth of timber wolf,
the understanding of elephant
and mammoth whales.
Or are you drawn by childhood fears
of killer sharks or giant crocs?
Jaws that sever flesh, yet awe inspire?

Or does the wild exist
for you in simple,
not such mighty things?
The trust of pigeon
feeding from your hand.
Dawn walks, through cobwebs spun
in dewy nets, damp clover,
a blade of grass,
a daisy half-awake?
Or resting in the shade
of sage oak trees
on balmy, summer days?

Maybe, you are drawn to a wild we cannot see?
The hidden world beneath our feet;
a realm of sprawling fungi, moles, earthworms, the woodlice,
burrowing field mice, the mini beasts, and all industrious ants?
The creeping spiders, slithering snakes – the tiny things
connected godlike and all-knowing to the soil.

How about the wild drawn as pitch-black night?
As we sleep – the beasts that bite;
Mosquitoes? Vampire bats?
Those that anesthetize
and suck their unsuspecting
victims' blood?

Or maybe wilderness is in an epic journey drawn;
the migrators –
Swifts that screeching dart
and hark from dark continents and never rest,
jet witnesses to the grunting communion
of a million grazing wildebeest.

Or traipsing frigid congregations;
the ungulates from colder climes –
a vision from the Pleistocene –
Porcupine caribou foraging
for lichen on icy North Slope trails,
whilst Arctic wolves play bloody tug of war
with a pathetic fresh calf foetus.
The survival of the fittest
stark in tooth and claw.

Or maybe – wild wonders come as less violent
migratory surprise.
A lone nightjar,
startled in torchlight on
an evening stroll in green hills?

It might be your eye is drawn to wild colour?
Then jewelled hummingbirds and vibrant butterflies
might be your thing?
And since we're flying high –
then what of the raptors – regal avian kings?
The soaring eagles, a buzzard's shriek that echoes primal
in the sky, the hawk that hovers above the moor –
a perfect crucifix in lofty overwatch –
and limber kite that swoop and spar.
Surely you are drawn to these wild things?

Or maybe your heart draws you beneath the waves?
To search for sentient octopus
in Grecian seas, or shoals of cod and herring
balls in boiling maelstrom pools
or the allure of tropical reefs, free diving in pacific blue?

Or is it cold immersion that you yearn? The wildest feeling
submerged in tannin Highland Lochs,
floating meandering rivers,
kayaking frozen fjords and sailing Southern Ocean swells
replete with broken shards of
icy berg that intrepid sailor so appals.

All wild nature – literally everything,
fascinates and draws me in.
Wilderness that grows relentless, sprawling free.
Amongst the hedgerows,
thriving beside motorway litter.
Surrounded on my walks in gentle hills in
pattering rain, remind me daily
of nature's majesty and of its pain.
The eerie wind that runs through talking trees,
up Downs, descending flinty paths in hot sun,
or a dewy morn; the frost covering an
unmown, autumn lawn.
All birdsong, rabbit scat caught between my toes.
The scent of pine sap, pungent undergrowth,
the waft of fresh muck spread on ploughed fields.
All these olfactory memories daily fill my mind
and build a three-dimensional sense in me
of being wild and truly free.

Whatever your cup of nature's tea –
one fact shines, most glaringly.

Dry Summer Rains

From the top of the hill fort
whiteness approached like
an incoming tide from the southwest.

Eight hundred feet below,
green forests remained green
arable fields scorched golden, hedgerows muted,

each slowly consumed by rolling mist
as fine spray pattered
and I closed my eyes,

willing downpour.
It had been a hot season.
And yet, the hills had not burnt.

And the jungly bracken,
thicker than I could remember,
soaked me as I swam towards my redoubt.

The pinetum had not burnt – not here, not this year.
Wildness prevailed. Cooler,
maintaining poise, embracing dry summer rains.

Extinction

Breath billowing,
we crept through a glittering,
subterranean lair.

In scan of torchlight,
Jarkov tusks, swept up to greet us,
magnificently from a block of woolly ice.

We marvelled
at each sepia point,
curled ivory twice the mass

of Africa's king,
and contemplated a lost world,
upon which giants reigned,

just four thousand years ago.
Whilst Mesopotamia so civilised,
on Siberian steppes, ancestor of Dolgan

hunted mammoth here and survived –
entirely on meat, hide and bones.
A tribal ecosystem yielded

from a single beast.
Now megafauna's relics,
stained by tundra tannins

and the peaty bog, were birthed, once more.
Thrust from glacial catacomb
by the warming of our time,

portended darkly to
extinction.
I fear the only rule.

Fall-fruit

Picking, barefoot
through rusting leaves
the apples rotting,
one snow white sat
magnificently hollowed.

Inside decay,
a ball of wasps,
gorged and burrowed.
Here, fall-fruit
nurtured,
nothing wasted.

Farewell

Home knows not
When we bid farewell,
Nor destination neither.

The rocks don't care
The sand and sea
But trees know

Animals, family
When we return.

Fear

For Greg

Go, go, go barked Craig.
I launched my bulk in giant
stride from transom through

bobbing aperture,
when carabiner on my
bandolier of paints

snagged upon wire mesh
as metallic 'snap' deafened.
Now well snared, half in –

half out of the cage,
my momentum pitched me head-
first submerged, in Cape

Seas as whitey now
turned ominously. Aghast,
Carcharodon at

flailing me, came full
speed, wake of froth beading off,
dull grey dorsal fin,

the stuff of nightmares.
Above the shouts on deck, my
brother's loudest heard

'No Bucky!' As gaff
hook in hand thrust he, towards
jaws of nemesis.

On sixpence did the
shark now turn, and with helping
hand, freely sank I

to contemplate the
Fear, that as torpedo came
through cloud of pinky

chum – to batter and
cajole. Yet with each pass, to
my own surprise, strange

emotion inside
grew. Childhood trepidation
of White Shark morphed to

simple wonder at
such a beautiful fish, the
'Perfect Predator'

lasting epitaph
seared profoundly in my heart.
My phobia, dead.

First Snow

At first, snow softens.
Drab brown quilted,
Birch stems glazed
In ornate kiss.

I push deeper. Shoulders
Shifting delicate balance, showered
Stumbling, until enveloped,
I stop and inhale deeply.

In this cold moment,
I am innately aware
My hot exhale
Ruins everything.

Forest Dance

For Lili

Act 1

Deep in pinetum,
Striding through a curl of mist,
Golden Larch is first to dance.
Brilliant, swirling, mustard glowing.

Next up, coerced
By the wind,
The floppy tops
Of Hemlock frolic.
Above evergreens,
And leaves burnt orange.
Limb tips lifting, then flattening,
Undulating in concert.

Act 2

Squall, now bolder,
Races through the sea of trees.
Amber embers of Deodar,
Birch and smouldering Spruce,
Urged aloft as fireflies,
Scalding Redwood littered soil.

Act 3

Soon the forest writhes
Ablaze, led in waltz,
Of fall's gilded creation.

Forests Slain

I drove north, past
Roadside forests slain,
Loamy soil all rutted
Muddy, soon overlain with
Tarmac. Trees' roots
Routed, dead trunks hacked
Pines piled rotting, bleeding sap
For yet more houses.

Frantic Fruit

Now is the frantic time.
Velvet damsons swell,
as sweet, barbed blackberry
probing tongues entice.

Cherry hawthorn fruit
do warn as cox ripe rotting
lure, then mottled plummet.
In the high branches, frenetic tit

and sparrow flit, pluck last
of summer wasp, gorge,
hop then bloated sit as below
industrious squirrel

and the field mice hoard.
Beechnut, a vast third-year crop,
Germanic bulbous acorn –
the hefted trove, soon covertly

buried in innate anticipation
as winter months simmer
inevitably. And so,
hour by hour,

day by day,
sultry morns are betrayed
by cooler dawns
and night-time blustery storms.

The tell-tale fall of rusty litter,
crunches brittle underfoot
until first frosts lattice
crumpled fields

all sparkling white
and I must too,
my hoard prepare –
for remorseless, darker times.

Freedom

Here, on eastern Altai
crag, endless wings
unfurled and
launched regally.

For the briefest of moments,
the raptor appeared, suspended.
Then a single flap;
effortlessly, gliding

up and up in alpine air
as wing tips carved
thermals and
hunter soared.

This was a godlike bird.
Fortified with all-seeing,
honey-coloured eye,
unfathomable to

scampering fox
below,
as malevolence
circled.

Then, trajectory
triangulated; eight talons
raised, ambush silent,
fur-ripping

scimitar beak
all bloodied, stabbing.
Brutal freedom roamed
this azure domain.

An arid wilderness
defined,
not by wolf or bear or man
but golden eagle's reign.

Gentleness

Through effervescent fumaroles
and currents powered by the moon,
silhouette of Leviathan
emerged, ominously.
Blocking out the sun.

This apparition evoked
in me a childhood dread
of predatory Carcharodon.
Yet, as shadows died,
a gentle, undulating giant
transpired.
Amethyst in hue,
delicately spotted,
maw cavernous,
yet not one serration
grew inside.

Emboldened,
we finned into blue.
Breathless astronauts in freefall
buffeted, by roiling undertow,
and dared caress
shark's rasping skin,
that emanated in
translucent glow.

Attempting to keep pace
with oscillating glide,
no time to plan or to compose.
Instead, spontaneous perspective
we now sought and so,
with frantic fingers,
moving over plywood board
our cobalt trace met graphite line.
In wonderment,
at whale shark's innate
gentleness.

(Artist's note, as honest marks upon
the page, as we have ever made.)

FIN
(The End)

Golden Song

Sitting on deadfall

surrounded

by golden song,

Nature spoke

gently.

Golden Stream

For Bear

Golden stream
Slips, gushing
Bubbling

Over shallows
Tumbling tiny
Rounded

Stones, as sandy
Sediment in
Sunlight

Plays. Here
By flood-worn
Bridge

We stop
To listen,
Moment

For a heartbeat
Frozen, before
Once more

Departing on
Our busy
Way.

Grace

1

Nemesis
kept distance in green waters,
before swirling closer.
Prehistoric apparition – passing
gracefully within inches,
blunt muzzle fixed in leer,
smile deceptive,
smuggling rows of killer's teeth.

I jammed my arm into
fissure of million-year-old berg,
for purchase in the swell
as sea leopard barrel rolled,
inquisitively,
whilst dive team tracked
serpentine movement in awe.
Behind misted masks,
inhaling deeply, our frigid fingers
gripped pencils urgently,
to scrawl trace of our encounter
beneath the ice.
Frozen senses fired.

Later, air expended,
hefted, as porpoise on Pelagic's aft,
I reflected on the awesomeness
of our encounter; five-fingered claws,
jaws designed to sever penguin and kill krill too,
this seals fluidity, pure perfection
as shivering my mind drifted
ominously, to our return across the Drake.

2

The sail south,
weeks earlier, had been terrible.
My 'salty' ego humbled,
unable to compute the undulating savagery
of rolling seasick valleys
fuelled by 'force ten up our chuff',
four days and nights. The nightmare endless.

Yet, buoyed strangely, by
the courtesy communicated
of this wondrous beast
that drew us over austere,
Antarctic seas,
far from clinched 'comfort zone'.
Yearning for my young family,
and home, had
a stark truth revealed.
That when adversities are shared
profound fraternity is forged.
The grace of wilderness, heart-swellingly restored.

Green Hills

You walk me, daily.
Up I amble, stony trail
Into the heart of

You. And here, alone
In your embrace, the green takes
Hold, and I get lost

And leave the trodden
Path and push willingly through
Bracken, bramble slash

A new trace, of my
Creation. Wildness here I
Find; mossy oak, straw

Grasses shining in
Islands of light. But it is
In cool canopy

I breathe deeply of
Your oxygen, roots birthed
Of rich, timeless soil

Undulating on
Layers of mulch and stone of
Ages past, the time

You grew, boggling
To comprehend. A life force
Of diversity.

Oh sanctuary
Of pine, and beech, hazel, larch
Fern, cairn and viewpoint

Such perspective adds.
And in so doing you, to
Me, become sacred.

Ground Truth from Kaktovik

Inspired by the words of
Robert Thompson

At the climate conference
In nineteen ninety-nine
Twenty-three scientists
Put their careers on the line

Declaring: Climate change is
Happening! I remember
Their words, their predictions.
Everything predicted, is happening.

Twenty-four years ago.
So little has been done.
Still, we're told we need more evidence.
The Inupiat need no more evidence.

Being rained on
In February, is evidence.
Polar bear declined by
Fifty-eight per cent.

Fish stocks along the entire
Yukon River are down.
No fishing allowed.
Fishing, in Western Alaska,

Has been devastated.
Knee-deep dead fish
On Kodiak. The crabs
Have left. We must

Take climate change seriously.
People are starting to,
Too little too late.
Young people are getting involved

They will, make a difference.
In Alaska, politicians are
Trying to drill more oil.
Here in Kaktovik,

I'm going to work to build
A 'zero fossil fuel' house.
I recall seeing a pile of
Forty-Two dead Caribou

Killed, by climate change.
Rain in the refuge in winter
Is gonna be hard on the sheep
Their food exposed,

Wind blows snow off it.
It's a beautiful day here.
Sunny, but cold.
I shall go for a walk.

Hallowed Ground

I sat, as still
As forest sits
Listening,
Sensing

Larch above
Me sway.
The light,
The sounds

The birds
The flies
The taiga's ways
The patterns that

Now met
My gaze
Beguiled me, calm
I'd found.

On mossy
Wet, yet
Hallowed
Ground.

Hawthorn

Today, I searched for wild
And found it.
Hawthorn charmed and then
Confounded.

Like bear I
Ambled into
Pliant thicket
Tricked, ensnared,

Scored, scarred,
Stabbed pleading,
Inveigled game trail left
Me bleeding.

Wild is not just
State of mind.
Enter thorn
And wild, you'll find!

Hello Light

For Dad

Tonight, I listened to my
Daughter
Sing words written by my
Father.
Sweet notes of
Hello light
Filled the night,
My darkness gone.

Hunted

I stand alone,
Naked, dripping wet, scanning
Sea of forest.

Lone wolf
Watches me, intently. Steaming
Breath, eyes jade green,

Soul piercing.
Then song, lamenting comes,
Rousing gathering.

I sense congregation
Within dark trees.
Padding of untrodden trails

Faint trace of paw,
Imprinted evidence
To bleed beneath

The icy crust.
I shiver. Hunted,
Skin goose white,

Joints stiffening,
Fingers blue, face flushed
Fight or flight?

I have no choice
I need this life
It beats within,

My will, fiery to survive.
And so, blade bared
I turn to face these

Hoary ghosts of taiga,
Barrens and the silvered plains.
Painting premonitions

Of my death.
Cerberus, soon carmine masked,
One body tugging,

Canines ripping,
Resolved to slash against my fate,
Yet strangely unafraid,

As Elk alarmed,
Steps out. Exhausted.
Damned to die.

I hadn't seen her
In the pines, close by,
My eyes untrained.

Doe's demise though
Savage, pleases me. Rather,
Her to die, than me.

I am Not Alone

I look about
As rain falls.

Surrounded
By rusted bracken,
Wilting white grasses,
Holly, and the birch.

Above tall trees
Harbour minibeasts
Unseen.

Beneath my feet fungi
Sprawling, interlaced.

And in grey skies,
Swells light of song
So sweet; chirps and twitters
Resonating everywhere.

Where roe roam
I am not alone.

I am home.

Ice Core

The glaciologist held
Translucent time-capsule
tenderly,
Between gloved hands.

Suspended, within
This gleaming yard;
Dark strata.
Irrefutable evidence

Of warmer days.
My gaze, settled
At ice-core's tip;
Grey sliver,

Flecked as ash
Upon a cigarette.
'How much trouble
Are we in?'

The field scientist paused,
As if digging, for his reply.
'All depends on what kind of
Nest we wish to build.'

Instinct

Cheetah gang lithe,
now stalked us.
Stealthily as grandmother's footsteps.

We turned to face the threat.
Their leader froze.
One by one the big cats watched.

No trick missed.
Silent scent, dog claw touch,
ear cocked, eye knowing,

alien investigation.
We knew what we were witnessing:
distilled predatory instinct.

To survive, we would need to sharpen
our own instinct,
and keep that weapon honed.

Invited

Invited, each
Bowed humbly,
Hug the tree.

To smell, to sense
The strength
To feel,

As pilgrims do,
What nature, forest
Means – to you.

Lair

In Winterfold
there is a lair.
Gashed

by claw
rain rutted,
tunnelled, filled with leaves.

I often sit here,
hidden by ancient yew
and contemplate

gouged outcrop;
how smoothed by time
mossed sandstone was,

this den,
the perfect place
for pups to raise.

Rock overhang,
the perfect seat
for wolf to gaze.

The yew knew.
He was old enough,
roots reverberating

wolf's padding,
trunk resonating
melancholic howling,

not just pack dog.
Thud and moan
of cave bear too,

I suspect these
old rocks knew.
For how wise is stone?

Compared to flesh and bone?
Skeletal trove
of prey devoured; antlers,

ankle bones, skulls all ground,
but lair remains, like yew,
I sense their secrets too.

Of wolf departed,
extinct bear
and burrowing beasts, anew.

Last Herd

1

First buffalo I ever saw
Ploughed headless,
Through thick quilt of snow,
Foraging wild grasses.

Steam rose from undulating,
Scruffy hump,
As cloud upon a mountain top.
Horned boss tossing up,

For glacial air, whilst
Mellow gruntings resonated.
This panorama,
Wafted, pungent of last herd.

Sunken trace, embossed
By hooves long-gone,
Still in evidence today,
Drew me, meandering

On my snow machine,
To vast Caldera.
Across frozen yellow river,
Through stands of Douglas fir,

Aspen and the cottonwoods,
Traversing blackened shards of
Lodge pole pine.
Before descending dell of

Sulphured geysers and
Boiling cobalt springs.
Shielded from harsh prairie wind,
By crown of icy alps.

2

In this frigid nursery,
Swollen beasts awaited.
Bloodied calves, soon spawned
As in dark trees wolf stalked, malevolently.

Here, I pondered sixty million slain,
In orgy, just six score before.
Parisienne predilections for plush hide,
Rendered fetid carcass littering,

Ribcages raven picked,
No rumination
On the endless plain
But near extinction.

Living migration metamorphosed
To pyramids of glaring skulls,
Of which the Pharaohs
Would be cruelly proud.

And I gave thanks,
For slipping glimpse of
This, surviving
Congregation.

Last herd protected,
By old Ulysses decree,
In solemn,
Perpetuity.

Loaded for Bear

Imagine, if you can,
Entering the alders
Loaded for Bear.

Vast tracks, pungent
Smell of scat,
Damp fur, a river mound

Ambling, just out of sight.
Hemlocks
Echoing misty moans,

The Great Bear's cough.
Prompting irrational fears.
Your blade drawn,

Heart pounding
Senses fired, remembering,
You're not insane.

Armed, instead by
What you've read;
Peacock, Strauss

And Stonorov
Mentors
To your soul.

Warning with words,
Not shots,
Why wild beasts matter.

Loneliness

1

George approached,
on horny toes, as Nureyev on points.
Stretching elephantine,
forelegs armoured, bony osteoderms,
skin mottled taut as drum,
aged by centuries of sun,
salt spray and arid climes, encased within
protective, heat regulation of his shell.

Then lolling, came his endless neck.
Topped with knowing fist-sized cranium.
With turtle's nostrils and beset
with kind, cognisant eyes.
The five-hundred-pound tortoise
floated in slow motion gait,
in warm reception of
spritely visitors.

We sat entranced, as triangular head bobbed,
contemplating this last remaining
icon of the Galapagos.
What joy and sadness had this gentle fellow witnessed,
in his lonely life?

From Darwin's touch,
to the extermination of his genus
by whalers, fur sealers a century before –
his kind believed extinct.

Then in Nineteen Seventy-One
on remote Pinta Isle,
József Vágvölgyi spied a single giant tortoise,
ambling across desolate, moraine.
That lone survivor was none other than
'Lonesome George'.
Living over sixty years,
Alone, unable to converse

in silent, secret code
with sisters, brothers, cousins,
parents and grandparents
long departed.
Bereft of companionship
but for feral goats
and blue-footed
boobies.

Yet despite great efforts
to regenerate
and breed his kind,
no mate was ever found
and in Two Thousand and Six,
George passed.
The last of his family
to ever tread this earth.

2

Walking past Victorian dioramas
of species stuffed
at The Natural History Museum
on my return,
I wondered of the last seconds of the gentle Dodo's life.
What might the last Red-Headed Indian Duck have seen,
flying in feathered squadrons over
vast herds of sixty million buffalo,

the resonant bugle of last Irish elk,
its twelve-foot palmated rack,
scythed in mortal combat with a marauding pack
of Dire wolves.

The bellowing fury
of the last cave bear…

How blessed was I to
have, a slipping moment shared
with such a venerable gentleman,
and survive, to tell his tale.

To my mind – George resides eternal –
weightless above his ancestral home.
His memory
Omen to us all.

Low Tide

The ripples came in waves
Seeping, not splashing
Across windless, Cornish sands.

Revealed in miniature dunes,
Lugworm scat abut a mace of kelp,
Barnacled pools still and clear

Home to rusty, scuttling crab,
Lank seaweed, neon glowing,
Strewn matted.
Imprints of dawn walker,

Track dog claw to
Ancient causeway,
Black stones
All lethal

Gleaming,
Daring passage to
the emerald mount,
Before tides turn.

Majesty

We staggered on, through
Blackened shards of last year's burn.
The steaming pile reminded us

We were not alone.
In this redoubt,
Amongst bowed birch

Beneath our trail, we
Heard crashing as Alaskan
Apparition strode boldly

Into light. Moose
Stood motionless, great
Equine head loomed,

Ears elliptical,
Palmated antler
Draped as rented battle flag

Victory bloodied,
Thrust from bony
Crown. Neck hoary, wallow

Of jowl leading
To great muscled
Hump, trailed through powerful

Shoulder down
Sinuous flank
Visceral and awesome to

Behold. Bull, then
Raised its velvet nose
In acceptance of our wind,

Before, once more,
Probing top crust
For tender willow

That cowered frozen.
We waited; Silence collaborative,
Senses tingling.

Our saga, primal.
To meet majestic beasts,
On foot. To co-exist.

Mangrove

Mangrove squats
On many legs;
Bastion to rotting logs
The archer fish,
Elusive rays
And dazzling shoals of anchovies.

But dappled tannins
Cannot mask, primordial
Lurking in our minds of
Knobbly, oscillating
Toothy things
We pray, we never find.

Meditation

Deeply
submerged,
beneath old Darwin's arch
we cling on, against
unfathomable surge
and meditate.
In and out
our mantra.
In and out
as bubbles swirl and rise.
Our focus,
to be calm,
to breathe,
simply to survive.

Mentors Gone

1

One killed Nazis.
A second commanded
Arctic Submarines.
Another taught the rhythm of
The rugby ball.
One the rhythm of the speed ball.

One knew art,
All art, and that I guess
Hooked me.
As did the one
Who walked with lion,
And understood the wildest things.

2

An artist from
An early age,
Mum drew with love
Upon the page:
Horses, flowers, all rural views
From gentle Kentish greensand lanes,
To tribal Mara's rutted
Black-cotton trails,
Her world,

so humbly shared,
In pen and Kodak colour slide.

Dad's craft
was also with a pen.
At Oxford University
A writer he became.

His words, inspired
Collaborative plays that
Resonated faith,
Mightier than all my,
Bruising, physicality.

3

Once, to my shame,
In adolescent rage,
I called Dad a fool…
But like the man
Who once was blind,
I now see, the fool was me.

So now, years past,
My mentors gone,
All wisdom gleaned,
I draw of wild I've seen,
And write of things
That to me, truly matter.

PS

Thank you, Mum,
And thank you Dad
The best mentors
this boy ever had.

Misool

For George

The mornings here
Brewed, wet clouds reflecting
Jagged as the backstrap of
A crocodile.

Most days it rained.
The lush green canopy
Fed, then rioting, coating steeples
Of coral rock.

Within these forested
Islands, rare orchid grew
Hidden from view
By shadows deeper

And more profound
Than the rarest azure,
Or cobalt blue
That interlaced, Misool.

Mustique Turtle

We finned, expectantly
across the milky blue,
between fishing boats, barnacled buoys
and twisted lines of past demise

And there, in this gentle bay,
just feet below, not one but ten,
horned angels flew, foraging
dappled pastures.

So down we dared, entranced
as green turtle glided up towards the sun,
and for the lasting of a submerged
breath did we, a twirling moment share.

My Daughter Kora

Crossing frozen swamp
I lost firm trail,
Soon bedded
Deeply, in a drift.

Unlike other years
In the North, this year
I was not alone.
Once small, now grown

My daughter Kora helped
Heave our sled,
As I waded, waist deep
Leading Ski-Doo

Like a digging dog.
Together we
Tugged then trudged
Connecting towbar

Soon speeding
As one, over snows
Through trees,
Towards home.

My Forest

1

Before me,
Lush bracken
Beckons.

In that jungly sea,
Staggered,
Like the legs of a huge beast,

Scots pines tiptoe
Through forest's carpet
To congregate.

It is dawn
And I am alone.
Aside from avian chorus

I feel at peace. My mobile off,
No sound of cars,
Or humanity at all

And that comforts me.
I allow the aroma of pine sap,
Verdant humidity of lush stems

And loamy soil
To wash over me.
The scent triggers anticipation,

A metalled tingle of adrenaline
I can taste in my mouth.
Olfactory senses working in tandem

With cerebral wiring
Jolting a deep-rooted
Muscle memory,

Palpable physical response
To danger.
The bark of distant deer,

Alerts.
Heartbeat pulses.
Then the echo of spring cuckoo

Makes me smile
And I inhale deeply.
Tuning in,

Aware of the journey, it has made
From Africa to my home
Thankful, for this beautiful song.

Vigilant,
I scan the forest floor.
Ahead sign, meandering

Through the Hurt,
Leads my eye.
I follow the game trail,

Below, low boughs,
And moments later
I have been swallowed,

Whole.
Secretly immersed,
I push through a wall of holly

To track fresh slots,
Around dead falls
Clad in turkey tail,

Through stands of head-high
Fern and onwards,
Into a clearing of amethyst heather

Where young gorse
And spindly birch riot.
Above me,

Old gentlemen tower.
Branches heavy
With tufts of olive foliage

Fist-sized pine cones
Reaching southwards
Orientating me

As I push deeper.
Cool air carries with it
Familiar sound.

A faint thrumming.
Great spotted woodpecker
Hammering territorial song

In hollow rotting
Of a lightning-struck larch
In search of grubs.

I step to the sound of
Drumming in between
Two Douglas firs.

There I spot movement,
And watch blurred cap
Of Indian red

Set atop banded wing.
Entranced by resilience
Of its skull,

I marvel.
Then swooping
Up, then down

He is gone.
On I push,
Willing the sounds and smells to

Flow over me as
Frenetic claws race vertically.
Grey squirrel launching

Balletically
Into coniferous canopy
And onto dancing finger

Of a lonely larch.
Then, heavier movement
As my quarry

Bounds
Chestnut, testing light.
For the briefest of moments

Roe and I share space
Once scented, Buck spooks

And in a bound is gone.

On a rise I stop,
Scan treetops and breathe deeply.
It is here, I hear it.

High above the chattering
Of crossbills and goldcrest,
The mellow cooing of pigeon

The desolate
Goshawk cries,
Echoing high above my forest.

I survey the azure sky,
Rare raptor floating
On thermals.

I watch him soar, and wonder
How hawk views me?
Ungainly lumberer,

Hundreds of feet below.
Do I even register
In his hunting ways?

I guess, I will never know.

2

The last brown bear
Roamed these wooded hills
More than nine centuries ago.
The last wolf, three.

By definition, this habitat,
In which I roam,
Might seem sanitised of wildness,
Compared to wilderness

I have known.
But it is not.
One hundred and
Sixty square miles

Of rolling pine,
Fir, larch, redwood, birch, oak and beech
More than suggest wild.
These stands of forest, left unchecked for years,

Emit the luxuriance
Of abundant biodiversity.
The key ingredients to life.
And I guess that is why I need their calm,

To bathe my body,
My mind, each day.
The Japanese have a name
For my daily ritual;

'Shinrin yoku' – forest bath.
Translated, 'to worship amongst the trees'.
The physical and mental benefits of
Simply 'being' amongst trees,

Thousands of years old.
No mystical
'Tree hugging' fantasy,
But hard science.

Dr Qing Li,
At Nippon University
Lists: reduced stress
Induced calm,

Lower pulse
And blood pressure,
Increased concentration, and creativity
Strengthened immune,

Improved quality of sleep
Reduction of stress,
And anxiety
Due to cortisol reduction.

All attributes of taking a daily
Forest bath.
But his research does not stop there.
On a molecular level

Friendly 'mycobacterium vaccae'
Found in forest soil,
Activate neurons responsible
For production of serotonin,

The chemical that promotes
Happiness and creativity.
Good reason artists, and poets
Take forest walks!

3

Of the Sixty-three thousand
Species classified
And two million organisms
Professor EO Wilson (Darwin's rightful heir),

Estimates a further
Eight million 'yet to be classified'
Organisms form our planet's biodiversity –
All still to be fully understood.

This data accentuates
The urgent need for us
To preserve all
Wild habitats especially,

Ancient forests.
There is another Japanese word
Referred in the west as 'Psithurism'.
The sound of wind whispering

Through the trees.
This mysterious forest voice speaks
To all who choose to listen.
It calms the mind – helps us connect

To nature and our primal.
Walking in forest
Gifts us more than
Physical health.

Being amongst the trees promotes
Our mental health.
Free therapy for everyone.
A natural 'reset' for our minds.

4

But there is more.
Forest is a symbiotic living,
Breathing, constantly dying,
Regenerating entity.

Oxford University
And Harvard attest
That trees indeed communicate,
Nurture family and move.

Some species up to fifty feet a year!
Pheromones
Are shared by trees on wind.
A tangible form of defensive communication.

We first learned this in Africa,
Acacia releasing tannins
To their leaves when kudu
Are sensed, browsing.

Unpalatable bark,
Thorny skin,
Generated internally by toxins
Dissuade creatures from doing harm.

Trees communicate with kin.
Below ground too. Interconnected,
By interlaced fungi which connects
Disparate roots via slow-moving electric pulses.

A web of sorts.
This communication
Is glacially slow
By Sapiens standards.

But electrical signals
Do travel up, through roots and trunks.
In this way trees, like us,
Give each other aid and sustenance,

In form of nutrients and water, even
To stumps of revered members of family.
A society can be judged
On how it treats the old and vulnerable.

Forest shines in this regard.

5

At this point in my tale
Mini beasts make their entrance.
Resident insects attracted, can be deployed
To attack invader or harmful hosts.

Like all things living,
Trees eventually die.
If allowed to rest in place
To 'mulch',

Trees will in turn,
Feed regrowth
Via nutrient Rich soil.
A beech tree takes:

Three hundred years to fully grow,
Three hundred years to die
Three hundred years to disappear –
A thousand-year legacy.

Throughout its life, it might produce
One billion beech nuts,
Shedding, every three years,
Feeding wild creatures and the soil.

Yet only one beech baby
Will prevail.
Food for thought.
And what of movement

I hear you say?
Almost all coniferous pines move northwards!
It takes a forest hundreds of years to edge
Towards the Pole

But thanks to wind,
Water, transient animals,
Seeds, and nuts
Indeed, some do translocate

To fall, bed and
Germinate in soil.
And so, the cycle of
Forest life continues.

Walking under forest canopy is akin
To living inside a gigantic,
Living, breathing
Carbon-ingesting creature.

Forest; the largest connected
Organism on our terraqueous earth.

6

And what of fantasy and folk tale?
Surely trees are godlike?
Worthy of our worship, since it is they who clean our air,
And help us breathe?

JR Tolkien was onto something,
For when amongst great trees
We are indeed amongst a power far greater
Than ourselves.

Akin to a cathedral,
Just more magnificent and complex
Than any built
By man's hand.

Recently out walking
With my daughter,
She asked me how we
Might protect our earth?

A deeply profound question,
Innocent, yet meant with all her heart.
I walked on in silence,
(Uncharacteristically for me),

Then I looked to the canopy,
For answers…

Natural History

Driving past the grand museum,
my gaze was drawn
between the banners
and the great façade,
to London plane trees
that stood, camouflaged.

I did not remember seeing
them before, but now, attuned,
I traced their peeling bark,
gnarled branches scrawled
as pencil on a papery sky
as feral pigeons glided by.

As horns blared and green turned red,
these old trees transported;
exploring vaulted catacombs
fossils, evidence of bird-sized
dragonflies, steaming swamps and
crocodiles that lurked at this, exact latitude

I realised now,
not architecture,
nor modern, man-made things
impress on me, the majesty,
or mystery of our
shared, Natural History.

Obsidian

For Daisy and Wylder

We left the concrete road and down
a storm-cut track,
Arion, our guide, navigating through
scraggy jungle dense with palm and

deadly Manchineel tree
until the brewing sky revealed a moorland scrub
that led to the summit of a hillock,
olive-thatched and scarred by rains, its leeward
face exposed in dark brown,
ochre soil.

Skirting this volcanic bay on foot,
Obsidian sand oozed smooth black between our toes,
The waves fury crashing, milky green,
a place still wild and still pristine.

Octopus House

I've visited you in many
diverse homes.
Wedged in rocky slabs submerged in cobalt
Greece, a plastic ice cream dome in Southern France
and at frigid Enterprise – beneath a berg,
ethereal red you flowed
to me alone.

Even in Londinium
at the British Museum,
your iconic beauty
does in glazed sepia,
ancient urns adorn.

At each house in which you dwell
you leave a tell-tale offering.
Your doorstep rich in littered shells and
tiny broken legs, and so a clue

to find, as we fin fleetingly
blocking out the sun.
Now in Mustique waters warm
a blanched Conch shell, my daughter's
latest find.

So patiently, with her cousin,
they await entranced,
as tapered, tentacle
delicately probes the turquoise light.
A sentience in eight
mauve limbs contained.

Thrilled, our congregated family
now floats, to spy your balletic form
morphing elegantly,
restricted only by the diameter of
what you see.
Your silky flushing, camouflaged
as inky cloud declares,
a creature of whom Poseidon would be rightly proud.

Ode to the Draw of the Wild

If we can dare admit there is no
'Us and them' but 'One and all',
then science can cease religious fight,
and esteemed Professors
can join the pantheon of Tribal Lords who, long before
the advent of a Christian world,
understood this ancient truth:

Our species is connected
brotherly,
to all things that breathe,
scamper, fly, tread,
swim or crawl.
And what fates await
the birds and bees,
the predators, all prey and life unseen,
the trees, the plants, rivers
and the oceans will, in time, befall us all.

And so, right here, right now
I vow solemnly,
with all my Viking soul
to fiercely love, defend and tell
of all things wild,
to which I'm drawn.
Oh, magnificent
terraqueous earth.
The centre of my universe.

'Til Valhalla' then,
or if you prefer, Amen.

Old Brown Water

Constantius fought Allectus across
Old brown water. Men cleaved, bled in slow flow
As downstream, in Londinium, pagans
Sacrificed, loved, died, and galleons sank.

Viking navigated old brown water.
Olaf slaughtering Benedictine monks,
Attaching ropes and tearing down London
Bridge, supports splintering, to drift away.

Later, old brown water reflected fire.
Bodies floating purple-pocked, plague-laved,
Empowered trade, the building of Empires.
Dark continents raped, greased by oily flow.

Today, I watched Labrador fetch and swim
Time after time, as relentless rain fell
Old brown water nonchalant, current strong
As tourists throng, coffee and phone in hands.

Old Man's Beard

At dusk I took a
Tuft of old man's
Beard and studied it.

Intricate, darkest
Green, woven
Lattice lightest

I'd ever seen,
And wondered
At this lichen's

Place to cleanse
The Arctic air,
Vital meal

Tea, delicacy
Of Moose and
The Reindeer.

One in a Billion

Hilltop here, where
Giants grow, stands largest
Pine that ever lived.

On same soil,
Great chestnut tree resides,
As old as Oak.

Single nut dropped
Did burrow,
Then took root,

Four hundred years ago.
Now knotted,
Gnarly gargoyle

Hewn, replete with
Warty burl and
Rifled fibres squat.

At immense base,
Husks are strewn.
I bend and cleave

A single nut, and
Contemplate;
Might this seed be

One in a billion,
To live, for millennium?

Outtavarra's Mystery

For Hasse, Jenny and Agne

We snowshoed
Idovouma's
Reindeer trail
Beneath stratospheric
Skies and resting
By a frozen swamp
Of staggered spruce
Outtavarra's mystery
Whispered to us
Through the trees.

'Build fire small'
Wind's wisdom said.
'Then add stouter
Limbs – but only
Once your tinder
Roars ablaze.'
So why, under
Kuormakka's
Stoic gaze did
I build fire big?

Inspired by
Kota maybe?
Or was it instant
Gratification?
Birch bark, of course,
Caught fast
But logs just smouldered,
So began 'baton'.
Charred hunks
Lined up, malleted

White birch
Feathered, slowly
Stacked as Jenga.
This time, flames danced;
Eating, breathing
Funnelling,
Glowing, golden hews
Sami lesson
Processed properly.
This ancient wood, understood.

Palisaded Plains

Rising to the sky, palisaded plains
Once were home, to buffalo alone.

Then from Wind River,
Came warring tribes.
Barbed arrows, flinty-tipped
Comanche, colliding fiercely
With native bands,
Later pioneers,

Trading mustangs, muskets,
Pox then steers –
Steely Rangers, soon learned art
Of war. Tough frontiersmen, prospectors,
Cavalry all closed in battle after battle but
Buffalo hunters' big 'fifties'

Ultimately counted final coup;
First people starved, then cleared.

Cutting north, barbed wire sang; rusting
Fiddle in high prairie wind, replacing rumination,
Along the Ninety-Eighth Meridian,
From Gulf to the Canadian.
Sweet grasses, fertile soil, Ogallala
Caprock cleaved for derricks,

Cotton, grape and grain.
My great-grandfather staked
His claim in same 'Staked plains'
Man's gain, again, stalking canyons,
Escarpment settled, privately partitioned,
Stolen Mesa's warring, all but done.

Penny Bun

Squatting under rusty fern,
amongst pine brash,
perfection emerges
patiently.

Nut brown cap
your leg so stout
flesh gleaming white,
no gill,
but milky sponge beneath.
You offer yourself
easily
from loamy soil.

Oh, Penny bun,
Porcini, Cep to some
to me, foraged gratefully,
the perfect forest meal.

Perception

We trudged, sodden,
stumbling over rotting branches,
the brush around us emanating
of mushrooms in the rain.

On a mulched birch stump,
Turkey tail grew, limpet-like
in tiny, spongy terraces –
the forest's oncology.

We stopped and inspected a circle of
Ink Caps – their network hidden
beneath the soil and wondered about
what lay beneath – unseen.

It was darker now, and colder than it had
been all summer,
autumn unstoppable
yet there ahead in the tunnel of trees,

shimmering and translucent,
a golden birch leaf waited,
suspended at chest height, in our path.
We circled, smiling – inspecting

our palms outstretched –
happy to explore our perceptions.
Here, hidden amongst these trees,
we had found nature's magic. It lay everywhere.

Petworth Park Oak

The park oak
Had grown
Into its own air.
Fingers fanned

Symmetrically, limbs
Stretching easy,
As far and wide as
Oak could ever grow.

No other tree
Dared shadow
Nor steal its light.
Roots splayed,

Centuries embedded
Impervious to wind
Fed by rain
Fallow scat

Mulching leaves
Torn twigs
As old as park trees
Grow yet, not immortal.

Pine Tea Shared

Today we walked
Trail, both known
And new.

Bracken wilted,
Birch cleared,
Sawn stumps,

Painted, brash fires
Smouldering
Yet undeterred, in

Acceptance we sat
Upon piney island
Amongst roots

Barred, marvelling
At forest. Here
We tasted

Two pine teas.
Aromas subtle, almost
Indecipherable.

By third cup
Profound lesson I had
Learned.

Not to complicate
Or overthink.
To trust instincts

Innately
The reason?
Age, all things

Matures.
Intensely.
So much better shared.

Pine Tree

For Kora

I do not see you grow.
Nor hear you cry
or feel your pain when
saw bites viciously.

I do not see you walk
or converse amongst your olive kin.
To me, you only whisper as I pass,
pushing heavily through your arms,

for once no words.
I sense you first, in early Spring.
Rub new sticky buds
between my index and my thumb.

Inhale deeply and fill my lungs of you.
Your serene elixir, My reward.
And sometimes, I mine for amber in your umber bark
to remind me of you,

when I am home.
Only amongst your kind, does my heart ever leap –
sometimes startled. As twig, brittle snaps.
Or scratching, razor claw resonates upon your hulk.

In these primal instants,
wild instinct drags me back
through ages past –
a place furred megafauna malevolently stalk,

a place I am hunter but also prey.
Until, as ridiculous antidote,
I spy a squirrel
scamper frenetically.

I watch as if defying gravity it tears,
before balletic launch to tangled arbours and freedom,
the monster in my mind slain
by simple realisation of our respective kind.

Later, as I get deeper lost
in your aromatic world,
my innate disquiet is further soothed.
Now sweet song fills the air,

as brilliant crossbill swarm
and chatter endlessly in the lattice of your residence
and finally, I smile.
Only you pave my loamy forest path – nothing lost.

Fallen needles downy, mattress-thick beneath my toes,
crisp cones strewn recklessly,
my pockets full,
soon tinder for my fire

when cold and darkness come.
Yet never do I see you grow.
Or walk or talk, or cry in pain,
exhale or cleanse my tainted breath.

But I know you do –
breathe deeply of me.
And in return, gift me exquisite air to breathe.
Watching calmly as I pass beneath.

Slowly, therefore, you live.
Stoic – your ancient breed.
Life giving. Swaying nobly,
as timeless murmur in the North wind.

Please, Please do not Drill Here…

So, it's back on.
Fracking, you say.
To set up camp,
To run barbed fence
Around ancient forest,
'Keep Out!' nailed
To bark of redwood family.

Then lumbering trucks,
Clog-sunken lanes,
Patrols of bored men,
The guard dogs,
The heavy lifting kit.

And one day, soon
Drills will bite,
Savaging roots,
Disturbing sleeping soil,
Obliterating mushrooms web,
The badgers' sets, the foxes too.

The moles and earthworms
And deeper still,
Penetrating hidden worlds
Of resting silt, Jurassic sediment.
Unknown secrets smothered
In the clay.

And far below our fragile earth,
You will inject your cocktail,
Toxic fluid flushing.
Now miniature quakes
Destroy all in their path.
Pollute the water table,
Impede regeneration,
Growth itself and all
We are yet to know.

And for what?
'Natural gas' you say,
A gas on which
Our children innately know,
We must no longer rely.
What you mean is 'Methane',
None more noxious
Released into our atmosphere…

Please, please do not drill here.

Primitive

Ahead, our Gurkha
Tracker froze.
Something, prehistoric
Lurked unseen.

Communication:
Hand signal, voice
Box disengaged,
Three sets of eyes

Scanning foliage
For feline trace
In misty Sal.
Then, at our toes,

Hari gestured.
Amongst leaf litter
Giant pug
Prints shone.

The tiger's
Flight path
Clear as day
Led us down,

In single file,
And willingly
We crept
Into maw of Luga,

Legendary tracks
Our allure, forged in
Bardia's mud.
For an age

On spoor
And parched, we
Marched, beneath cornice
Carved by a thousand

Monsoons.
Then above, bush
Exploded.
Violent roars,

Showering us
In riot of wild
Shrubbery.
Breath held, hearts pounding,

Tiger battled
Bengal Bagh.
Instinctively – Suze
Reached, for a river rock

As I, my Kukri drew.
So, this was how
Our end
Would come?

Primitive,
Would we three
Die. Then smile cut
Hari's handsome face.

'Tiger mating'
Came whisper,
With a grin. We spied
Brief glimpse

As orange
Melted olive.
This day,
We truly lived.

Primordial

It lay deflated on mudflats in the
shade of white gum trees.
A century waiting.

In the shallows
we bobbed. Contemplating the vast reptile,
unchanged since

Cretaceous.
Puce jaw more rotting bow
than breathing dinosaur,
replete with yellow daggers.

On its spine
row upon row of grey nodules
studded five foot wide,
A knobbly pontoon

Capable of ferrying a child across
the sliding chocolate Adelaide.
We watched, reptilian eye for

flicker, hand-like claws, girth oozing,
A hulk of matter forged of time.
But Marakai did only watch

Lime green eyes
nonchalant, not one blink,
in ancient ambush.

Rain's Path

The rain's path
Slithers
Through lifeless
Leaves.

What once was up,
Is now down.
Green turned brown.
Sodden carpet cleaved

As rocks and roots
Slip deadly underfoot.
I follow nature's trail.
Not lost,

My mind meandering.
Fired by earliest
Yearnings, on the farm.
I now stand,

Bow in hand,
My little brother helmeted –
Close behind.
First kills witnessed,

The rabbits jerking,
Hind legs thrumming in my mind.
Leaking life upon
Old LandRover's metalled floor,

As leaden pills scatter,
Reckless in the dash.
And climbing trees,
Any tree,

Tunnelling to Australia,
Imagined worlds,
A place where nature
Magicked the impossible.

Boundaries – there were none.
Aside from impenetrable bramble,
In the bottom field.
Yet here too,

We, our battles, won.
Happy tongues, stained purple
With ripe blackberry.
Our spirits, running free.

In those days,
Shod in muddied hiking boots
As now, always afoot,
I carried my knife,

My life, as Viking
Strapped upon my hip,
Dreaming always.
Here in converted Oast

Between our bunks,
Dog fox contemplated rooster.
Beasts of folklore
My guardians,

As I soundly slept.
The murmuring of mum and dad
Lulling, yet always greedy
For the morn.

The certainty of dawn;
Of breaded ham and eggs.
Rissoles spitting fat,
Smells wafting

Delicious, nutritious,
Prepared by Grandpa's
Expert butcher's hand.
Then, on with wellies

And Anoraks.
Mucking Eiger,
The Bouquet of dung,
Old brindle Ridge,

Bull-faced and slobbering
Happy on his steaming throne.
Our mum, kind and loving
Nature burning bright

Within her hazel gaze.
A memory, I yearn to touch…

And so, half a century past
I stand. No longer boy,
But heavy-bearded man
With adult kids and wife.

The world I've seen,
Wilderness on every land
And sea,
Those beasts I dreamt of

Earned.
Yet today, of all days,
Rain's path
Urges me to truly see.

Rain, such familiar entity,
Passing in waves,
Turns the water.
Amber kayaks

Eddy on ripples blown
By wind.
A Minnow,
No Great White,

Cuts surface, then slips from view
As apparition.
At lake's far end,
In the reeds,

Impasse of willows thrust,
Pliant yet defiant.
Defending hidden things.
The beyond,

Now awaits.
Not the past.
The future,
I cannot tell.

Beyond, forest rests
Wet and glorious,
Urging me full circle
To embrace the now.

Recce to
Axel Heiberg

We flew, due North.
Four rotors thudding.
Low level, whooping
In excitement,

Gripping door gunner's
Webbing, contouring
Ellesmere's retreating
Glaciers, sediment

Carved by ages.
Tundra tussocks
Flecked, with survivors
Of the Pleistocene;

Musk oxen, gleaming hares
The size of spaniels.
Marauding Arctic wolves.
Landing atop a bluff,

Our team chattering
In awe-filled
Québécois,
Disgorged upon

Loamy Eocene
Surrounding stumps,
Remnant of dawn
Redwood,

Cypress, air-dried,
Mummified,
Preserved pine,
Gingko, balls of

Amber resonating,
Between our fingers.
Evidence of forty-million-
Year-old swamp.

Alligator, turtle
Thriving in proximity
To the Pole.
Witnesses to a warmer world.

Before Ice Ages,
Before man.

Regiment

Regiment of
Day-Glow tubing
Stood to, shielding
Stems of oak.

Insurgent Roe still
Skirmish, browsing.
Forest severed till,
Resown.

Sea's Fury

The explosion came
Just before the dawn.
Crashing against dreams
Alerting me
To Sea's fury.

I lay drifting
In a no man's land,
The waves no better
Understood.

Unfathomable power
Roiling me in slumber,
Amongst the pebbles
And the greasy undertow,

Drowning, slowly.

Secret Lives

What we know of animals,
And their secret lives, can be written
On a postage stamp.

The baby hippo greeting
Giraffe, long neck shielding
As its own child.

Tarantula, protecting
Frogs, who in return
Nurse, their spider's spawn.

Green woodpecker, gifting
flight to weasel. The tiger shark,
Yearning, for a human's touch.

Polar bear adapting,
To a warming world
Angling, needs must, in melting residue

To share bone pile and later mate, with grizzly sow.
Leopard that befriends the village dog,
Lioness that orphaned faun adopts.

Fraternity of fishes on the reef,
The blue illuminated by the ways of moon,
The octopus cerebral king, shapeshifting.

Empathy we rarely see,
The forest nurturing decaying family, the myriad
Of secret lives of trees,

Animals and those that fly and
Swim; the whales and krill
That daily interact, and always will.

Secrets of the Land

Today I trod old trail alive.
Through forest severed,
On I persevered.
Until light distracted,
Through blonde grasses
And I lost my way…

The Sami, know
Secrets of the land.
Each reindeer's track,
Each rock,
Each mossy coated tree,
Intimately.
And so, in reverence,
I retraced my steps, willingly.

Why?
Because some things
Matter more than others.
The seasons' changing ways,
All creatures too,
The clouds and stars

Currents, tides, the old, old ways.
These things we do well to learn,
Not master, mind.

PS I found my trail,
and survived to tell this tale.

Shadow Over Moor

Shadow, shimmered
Over endless moor, morphing
Before fleeing,
Blushing skies.

I tracked this sleekness;
Contouring bare hills,
Undulating across grasslands
Shapeshifting in congregation

Of tiny feathers that
Sang as purl, murmuring
Songs of winter. This most magical
Of clouds, inspired in me wonder,

Wonder at each glossy bird,
Creating change in seven others.
What change could I create?
As I drove south.

Shoreham Gap

From the tower
Sea shimmered,
Like a silver coin.

The Sun playing,
Just out of reach,
Beyond grey hills.

Snows of Amber and Gold

The wind whipped
the birch in waves,
leaves cascading in snows
of amber and gold.
High in a darkening sky,
gunmetal clouds wrought
the heaviest of rain.
Change was coming,
and all trees understood.

Spirit

Rocks have spirit,
Trees have spirit
And the air we breathe.

Animals have spirit,
Birds have spirit
And all crawling insects.

Rivers have spirit,
Ocean has spirit
And all fishes.

Our forefathers understood
Nature's spirit.
To take only what we need.

Sunrise

For Her Majesty

The new day
emerged slowly.
The grass greener than
I remembered.
The sands velvety,
the water shimmering
the rarest silver.

On the mount,
black shadows
carved new dimensions
in the trees.
The storm smoothed rocks
glowed golden,
the lone cedar silhouetted
in tribute against an eggshell sky.

This sunrise was regal.
Even the soaring gull's wing tips
dipped in reverence,
horses bowed their great maned heads along the beach
in remembrance of their kind champion.
A great spirit had passed
and all nature knew it.

The Great Bear
Listening to an Iroquois legend

For Oren

I first pondered
your congregation
on a cold, clear night in January,
many moons ago.

Alone,
I scanned the heavens for
Polaris but instead,
my gaze settled
on your twinkling dipper.

Much Later, I learned from a man
with a big degree (much wiser than me),
Merak and Dubhe aligned perfectly,
steering me North.
He told me your winking constellation,
reverberated with star music.

But back then, living deep in Iroquois
territory, I had simply wondered,
whom else had you guided?
And the stars had answered…

The boxing gym, seven storeys up
the Niagara Mohawk building, on the
corner of Erie Boulevard proved
a serendipitous rendezvous.

Trudging grey Up-State snows,
my nightly pilgrimage downtown
revealed your people's iconography
strewn everywhere. Appropriated,

not gifted –
a legacy confined to the Res,
wall plaques and ice-rimed manhole covers
but strangely alive in your calm words.
'Right jab, left cross, switch and move'
Oren in my corner: skills relayed from
master to apprentice – despite
Lacrosse being your warring game,
I had listened. Inspired,

by your manner
to search deeper,
to understand a pre-Christian world
where creatures were all brothers, dinner and gods.

To seek out creation stories.
The blood clot and the hare and
The hunt for the Great Bear.
Lessons whispered from an ancient past.

Your story is meant to be spoken.
Conveyed
in Faithkeeper's breath,
to be passed down, to aid survival –
lessons innately practical and spiritual.

Tales told long before Thor rode his chariot
across the night sky.
Before the first snows of winter.
Before the first autumn.
Then there had been just tribe
and endless forest –
The Great Turtle Island.

So, now might be my time to tell
the story Oren never told.
The story I discovered for myself
but fear is not mine to tell.

Yet, write I did
until conflicted, my wife encouraged me
once more to go search of Oren's council.
And so, I pressed send.

A month passed, then one starry night
sitting in my car, via new-fangled inventions
I once more heard
the gravelly tone of my old coach –
now ninety years of age.

And after warm pleasantries
bridging thirty years
we discussed the story.
Both relaxed approval and
creative criticism,
a request for me to edit,
redraft with preface
to place his nation
front and centre.

Then, as our conversation
meandered, a wounded fury echoed from within
the hand-hewn timbers
of Oren's redoubt –
flowing across big water,
piercing my heart.

And I listened
to his anguish:
that a Papal decree,
issued over six centuries ago,
afforded his people the mere rights
as the hares, foxes and crickets –
a profoundly spiritual people subjugated for all eternity
by an intolerant God.
Never rescinded.

And what I heard,
made me profoundly ashamed.
And I vowed to my friend to stand in his corner, as he
had in mine.
And honour that, which I do not own,
for all time.

The Hyena

The hyena snapped.
Broken jaw tiring,
Toothy grin
Pain-tightened,
Wounds infested,
Battling, the inevitability
Of vulture with all its
Howling soul.

Soon life left it.
The squabbling begun.
Yet despite
Bitter debate,
No flesh, nor bones
Were wasted.
Everything wild,
Would feed.

The Introduction

Funny old thing, introductions.
Especially to family,
Family as old as mine.

Like most first greetings
A hug is best if you want
To bare your soul that is.

A hug gives. A hug feels.
A hug shows you care.
Your willingness,

Showed me you care.
About looming family,
Red skin wrinkled, soft, like

Folds of warm air.
The smell of their hair
Their girth, their strength.

Thank you for coming
To meet my family,
For showing me, you care.

The Lost Herd

For Jason and Patty

Wind River Reservation, Wyoming

Ahead the land rolled away in front of us; the sky endless, the brush dotted with mustard flecks of pronghorn, the wind fragrant. The road meandered up onto a high mountain plateau; more antelope, seas of sage, crooked fence posts woven with staggered lengths of rusting wire that edged the undulating prairie. As we drove down the main reservation road towards Lander, through a break in the low cloud base, we were confronted by a glimpse of the snow-capped tops of the Wind River range and the gateway to hidden high, wild country. The pick-up turned abruptly, then jolted down a muddied track. We followed. The flinty trail led us down a steep rise and there we skidded to a stop. A hundred yards in front, in the creek bottom, a buffalo and calf grazed on the wild prairie grasses. Jason ambled towards our truck, smiling kindly. 'First time in one hundred and thirty-one years buffalo hooves have trodden this ground. It's a great day to see buffalo!' The thickset Shoshone turned to observe the mother and calf. Patty, Jason's wife, slipped out of the side door, then drifted from the vehicle and sat on a rise and watched quietly, as a dozen or so buffalo emerged from the brush and began to approach. The buffalo kept on up the rise, passing within a few feet, and congregated twenty head strong on the bluff. We began to draw a chocolate, heavy-horned male. Jason watched us from behind. 'The big bull, we call him "Thunder".' His name was fitting. A vast hump and deep chest, curved horns and a great furred boss beset with bright eyes framed with jet lashes... one of the most impressive creatures we had ever seen. This buffalo reminded me of a Yoruba poem I had stumbled across in Seamus Heaney's *The Rattle Bag*: 'When you hear thunder without rain it is the buffalo approaching.' Buffalo were back on Wind River – as natural a sight as anything we had ever witnessed in the bush. As essential a component of this ancient land as the flinty rocks, the cloying mud, flagrant sage and swaying sweet grasses. Their scruffy, umber pelage melted perfectly into the landscape. Their cloven hoof prints pitted every inch of soil. Their gentle, non-destructive browsing and relentless roaming were fertilising the land before our eyes. Here, buffalo were doing what buffalo do: trampling shoots of invasive aspen, opening up the prairie to its former glory. We got Jason and Patty's vision. It enveloped us. We heard it on the wind, we smelt it. Our audible and olfactory senses coaxed by gentle ruminating, snorts of indignation and the musky perfume of the buffalo's natural fertiliser as steaming chips wafted. This was buffalo country pure and simple. The lost herd had returned. Finally, the balance of this sacred land was to be restored. We were witnessing the beginning of something magnificent.

The Oldest Oak

The black cloud clamoured
on the wind.
Swooping.
Unfurling.
Squabbling in parliament
above the oldest Oak.

A thousand spiny nests
studded that canopy.
Below a stout building,
crumpled skin folded by ages
and countless storms,
hacked by axe, that had shattered,
not up to the task.

Their treasure though,
remained safe.
Warm gems in speckled hues of
green and blue, cosseted in
softest lamb's wool and
woven roe hair.

What rose before me
was a miracle.
Magnificent avian ecosystem
spawned by a humble acorn,
a millennium growing.

The Stop Line

At Blatchford
Concrete, brittle
Brick decayed as
Red birch,

Rosehip interplayed.
Here, bramble
Rusted wire
Entangled,

Re-enforced bunker
Ruminating.
Eighty years of
Resting, waiting.

The Storm

1

Rain marched across the land.
In extended line,
Flattening tinder
Drenching, cascading
Down, as I crouched
In lee of ancient Yew.
I was armed and prepared.
Flat cap off, in remembrance.
Hair flowing, beard wild
Urging salvation
In the mire.

2

The next morning
The trail was all died up.
The soil thirsty
As it lay, processing
The sheer weight of the water.
And I, the weight of dreams
Both thought and memory.
Those two Ravens shifting,
Disguised as Rooks,
In commotion upon
Norse wind.

The Wind

Last night wind
Penetrated
My dreams. The timbers
Of our cabin heaved
And groaned,
The black spruce
Writhing as if furious,
This land reminding
Us it was still wild –
And we, still human.

In the pink light of
Dawn, wrapped in wool
I crept outside to sense
The storm.
To my surprise, wind blew warm,
Pressing gently against my
Face, whispering in gusts
Strong enough
To cajole lichen
As sage, tumbling
Over twig-littered snow.

The Wren

The wren skitters,
nut brown,

weaving through rose hips
burnt autumn orange,

taunting within phalanx
of thorn.

Above buzzard soars silent,
as raven cronks warning.

Yet wren is happy.
To be wren.

Tolerance

The great bear ambled
Stiff legged, towards our truck and
Craned up at us. Wedge-

Shaped head so close we
Could taste his meaty breath. Jet
Eyes penetrated.

Battle-scarred muzzle
Jutted, moist nose twitched – possessed
Of a life of its

Own. I wondered what
He made of us? Trespassers
To his Arctic home.

And what might occur
If we were to clamber down,
Onto the food chain?

The very next day
We found our answer. Yard by
yard, on foot, we closed.

Nanook licked Hudson
Bay wind, as spindrift melted
On hot black tongue. Then

Slumped heavy on fat
Haunches. This bear's bearing spoke
Not of homicide

But strange tolerance.
We both held our nerve, aware.
Then began to draw.

To Survive

Hyena, poisoned
Battling vulture.
Polar bear, foraging,
Iceless shale.
Caribou, piled frozen,
Mounded
Turtle wrapped,
In nylon line.
Orangutan dazed,
Bereft of jungle.
Nature bawling,
To survive.

To Write a Poem

For Lucy

Write of what you sense,
what you hear and taste and smell.
Write of what you feel, both underfoot
and passing through the trees.
Write of all you see, emotionally.

Track

At our feet
Dragonfly hovered,

Over a story in two halves.
The track elliptical, all telling.

We froze
In Selous heat,

As tsetse strafed, cicada droned
But not one word did we utter.

We tested our wind,
Ash scattered, swirling

In gentle gusts against thankful cheeks.
Snowfall pattering hot grasses.

'Nyati hapa!'
Festo whispered.

Voice box disengaged.
Eyes laser-focused on suicide bush,

Not twenty yards ahead.
Then Rigby swung to shoulder

As foliage undulated.
Bolt, worn silky smooth,

Rammed round
Into battery.

Made ready, we skirmished forwards
Stealthily,

Tick birds
Chattering feverishly,

As crumpled boss of
Dagga boy reared into view.

Here we stopped.
Respecting distance

As our adrenaline coursed.
Back in the zone, every fibre

Electrified.
Hearts pounding.

Tracking dangerous game on foot.
The rarefied drug we craved.

Trepidation

Jesus took the lead,
methodically
probing.

In trepidation
we followed.
Scanning the abundance;

water lilies, marshwort,
chaotic roots and vines
spongy beneath

bare toes,
as Bubba caiman slithered.
High, in the sky,

Llano's vultures spiralled,
casting shadows over ocelot and
elusive El Tigre.

But we had not journeyed
far to track those cats.
And so, knee deep we waded,

alert, until mud
oscillated.
Then lighting stab

of fang,
the huge green snake
roiled up, then disappeared

below the cloudy soup.
Our guide now boldly
plunged his fist,

down deep as thrashing,
anaconda
emerged enraged.

Its wedged head
held vice-like,
Jesus nodding urgently

for me to grasp
the lethal jaws
as Suze controlled

lashing tail.
With our undulating cargo
we three staggered,

in single file
towards hard-packed clay
and refuge of a hessian sack.

Ours, strange collaboration
of art and science.
The anaconda calm,

as genetic code was
delicately drawn by
learned hands

soon released,
to slither free.
Muddy residue,

sole epitaph
to our most magnificent,
encounter.

Truth

One night,
trudging to our camp,
a wail wafted to
us longingly through the trees.

I retorted in
my simian howl, and to
our surprise,
wolf brother spoke
close by.

We bathed
the forest in torchlight and
there, not twenty yards
away, timber wolf
sat, reddish on his haunches
surrounded by a
pile of beaver
dragged into cover
at the base of pine.

This wolf emanated
a wild crackling
of vitality
that bridged the gap
between two species and
coursed electric through our veins.

Taut through
hoary shoulder, wolf muscles
rippled, moist nose glinted, ears
pointed long – all hearing,
as wide-set almond eyes
watched us –
burning with sentience.

This was the big, bad
wolf of Folklore.

The wolf I
conjured in my mind as a
child,
a wolf that could
gobble granny whole!

We watched him for an age, till
batteries died and traced
the primal imprint
Of our close encounter
upon our paper.

Our 'truth'
the most cherished
memory of all.

Twenty Fat Fridges

Walking through a stand
Of mossy oaks,
That I regard as friends,
Twenty fat fridges sat, abandoned.

Their whiteness, rusted
At the seams left a chill,
In me, as if I had climbed inside,
Not seeing red, but instead

Understanding, that whoever
Had tipped them here,
Had never walked amongst my friends,
And felt bracken wet against their legs,

Or heard birdsong sweet or parted
Morning mists that fed the moss,
Nor marvelled as light played
Through translucent leaves.

Two Lovers

Looking through
leaded pane, rain
sheeted, as wind whipped
reddish leaves in maelstrom.

In that autumnal bluster,
two black birds did muster,
colliding, frantic
dusky feathers

intertwined both floating,
weightless
in wild air,
before alighting,

two lovers paired
before departing.

Understanding

One morning, we came
upon fresh elephant spoor
in the gritty sand.

It emanated.
Adjacent in the ochre
soil, sign betrayed

prehistoric tracks
I struggled to encircle
with my arms. Finely

etched, hot we followed,
dimensions raised into light.
Meandering we

marched along the brown
Ewaso Ng'iro did in
silent thorn, spy bass

reverberation
with our ears. Our camel train
not one Bunduki,

or Safari car
in support. On blistered shanks
we trod, brutal mile

on mile – endowed of
Samburu skill. Yet, tracking
as grey Acacia

shadow browsed, then melted,
made all the sense in the world.
We felt no fear, just

profound awareness
and helpings of awe. Instead,
of cigar-sized six

hundred, I plucked a
single graphite stub. As we
bowed to draw, to my

impressionable
mind; Karamoja and Bror
might to African

skies have raised their eyes.
But this bull understood
our intention.

To paint and
not to kill.
In that moment,

our life's mission,
innately sensed.
Bush now our studio.

Vakkara

For Kenth and Ann

At blistering pace,
Through glowing
Night, my friend
Negotiated
Undulating
Trail worn smooth,
Passed endless birch
Blurred gateway to vast
Frozen lake,
And twinkling
On far northern shore
Slept Vakkara.

So, with friends, family
We drank and ate.
Horned cups full,
Reminiscing
Axe-hewn logs
Reverberating
Wind, memories
Reminding us
Of why we yearly
Journey North,
And why we love
This Arctic place.

Vision Quest

For Kubaan

Damp, deceived,
Blindfolded we huddle
Bucking in the bakkie.
Then truck halts, abruptly.

Led roughly, bastard thorn
Stab blistered feet,
Veldt's grey dusk
Thick, with terrifying sounds.

Now, Tarkie 'tracking stick'
In dirt, defines my world.
I grasp gnarled deadfall,
Gruff Dutch muttered

Match head, raw egg
Traded, as staff melt and
Darkness cloaks.
'Op's Lonesome' begun.

First fire, one strike,
Vasbyt,
My heart jumps
As scrabbled grasses

Dance. Flames warm
Across cold face
I lie awake, shivering.
For camaraderie

Whoop of hyena
Skirmishes closer,
Then smashing, screaming,
Howling comes

My mind ablaze with monsters
Some imagined, most not,
As Southern Cross
Blinks, exhausted eyelids fold

So, slumber comes.
Now dawn creeps
Frigid, embers dead
But I don't care,

I've klupped first night,
Survived scout's
Test. Half buried, filthy
In this ochre dust,

Firm egg delicious,
Munching, then comes thirst.
Now broiling sun becomes
Tormentor, tracks

Of predator surround,
As I reside, inside,
Sand circle.
By second dusk,

I've been reborn.
Humbled by this wilderness,
Bush, I thought I knew,
My vision quest, begun.

Water Walking

Water, walking,
always seems to find a way,

Through leaves,
Sand, mud and even cloying clay.

I must be as water flowing,
Always walking, to find my way.

West Wittering

For George

Mud.

Lapping, led us
Skirt-stunted, salty
Oaks, onto strand

Of sand. The dunes leading
Into light. Fragile razor
Grasses swaying,

The wind warm.
Air clean. Here we stripped and
Ran – tide in.

Over rippled ridges,
Ropes of lush seaweed
And tiny shells

Avoiding pebbles, splashing
Waist deep, rubbing mud.
Exfoliating, unaware

That in our happy hands
We held sea's secret;
A sacred sludge that captures,

Transforms the dead,
Cleanses air, oxygenates,
Regenerates.

Mud, misunderstood.

'What Astonishment!'
For Sir David Attenborough

Watching Sir David,
Witness, as a child,
Manx Shearwater

Hatching, upon
Skomer's weathered
Rock, first flap,

Then fly, across the sky
Over sea,
For eternity,

Then battle back
To that exact
Welsh outcrop.

'What astonishment!'
Indeed, our wondrous
Life on earth.

Thank you,
Nature's champion.
For always being you.

When I Die

When I die, I want
To be eaten by an eagle.

Flown across the world,
Across the forests, the seas

Over mountains.

When I die, I want to be fed
Back to the earth.

White Down Lease

1

At White Down Lease,
The Yew's thrust
Thrumming.
Branches, trunks
Hollow, drumming.

2

These coiled roots
Resonated, languid
As an anaconda's hulk.
Glistening, thick and
Just as smooth,
As finches in their
Concert flew.

White Horses

For Hussain

Now currents urged us
Down, into idyllic realms
Where neon anemone
And blanched trees
Fanned, wafting ornately
As we passed.

Here, upon live lattice,
Just out of sight,
Minuscule white horses grazed
As turtles fed,
Clown fish lurking
Beneath a clam so old
As to be unfathomable.

Wild Grasses

What makes the wild grasses grow?
Pastures parched, downtrodden.
Arid soil as tough as tarmac.

Then, eventually, rain and
cooler morning dew. Growth, simmering
unseen but damned slowly.

First gill of beefy mushroom,
a buttercup reaching, the clover matted
as you emerge, green shoots sprouting

impossibly through hard-baked crust,
before your amassed clans congregate
and break out in riot.

And in the wilder places – grasses reedy
and straw coloured, fine with seed as light as summer wind
wave, wilting towards the sun.

Where barren summer turf once reigned,
your lush carpet now prevails.
Autumn's order rightfully restored.

Wind Blew

For Mum

As rain fell
Emotions well, as wind blew
I talked to you.

Words of Wildness

I am not concerned
with perfect poetry.
I am concerned
with words of wildness.

Wilderness
speaks profoundly,
if we choose to listen.
To our myriad senses,
and the sixth,
innately tuned.

Ground truth,
foraged walking
come rain or shine,
snow or sultry summer heat
to be painted
upon the page.

My duty?
To warn and to be truthful,
as poets must.
To share with you
as nature,
shares with me.

Words

Only once my book
Was put to bed,

I realised what
I hunted.

Words, emotions
How I feel,

What whispers,
Nature mutters

What truth the
Wild utters.

FOR BEAR AND KORA

This book is dedicated to all the creatures, both great and small, it has been my fortune to encounter in the wild, and to my mentors who have guided me, inspired me and taught me in my quest to explore, paint and understand wilderness.

To my wonderful Mum and Dad who fostered my love of wild animals and distant lands, and encouraged me to follow my dreams and live the life of my choice.

To my wife Lisa and our kids Bear and Kora, you are my 'Why'. Thank you for your love and for sharing a deep love of nature and many of these journeys.

To my brother Greg for your talent, generosity and support over the years, and to Mike Bone and all the team at GWP for your beautiful design and care in helping to create this book.

To Suzi for over thirty years of artistic collaboration as my expedition partner, and for your unwavering friendship and wisdom.

Olly Williams

ABOUT THE AUTHOR

Olly Williams is an artist, writer and conservationist. This is his first collection of poetry.

For the past thirty-three years Olly has worked in wild and remote regions of the world, documenting the plight of the endangered predators, predominantly in painting and drawing with his collaborative art-making partner Suzi Winstanley.

He lives with his family in West Sussex and Arctic Sweden.

To learn more about @ollysuzi and their work in the wild, visit ollysuzi.com.